THE SUCCESSFUL DREAMER

HOW TO UNAPOLOGETICALLY LIVE YOUR TRUTH

MATTHEW C. HORNE

Lightning Fast Book Publishing, LLC
P.O. Box 441328
Fort Washington, MD 20744
www.lfbookpublishing.com

All rights reserved. No part of this book may be reproduced or transmitted in any form or by any means—electronic, mechanical, photocopying, recording, or otherwise—without the written permission from the author, except for the inclusion of brief quotations in a review.

The author of this book provides strategies for successfully living your dreams. The literary offering provided is non-fictional and derived from the experiences and message of the author. In the event that you use or implement any of the material in this book, the author and publisher assume no responsibility for your actions.

The publisher, Lightning Fast Book Publishing, assumes no responsibility for any content presented in this book.

Copyright © 2020
Matthew C. Horne.
All rights reserved.

ISBN-13: 978-0-9994653-9-4

TABLE OF CONTENTS

Dedication 1

Preface 3

Chapter 1: Be Sold On Yourself 5

Chapter 2: The Short Account 15

Chapter 3: Acknowledge or Accept 29

Chapter 4: The Never Ending Faucet 41

Chapter 5: The Financial Lifestyle of the Dreamer 51

Chapter 6: How to Escape the Matrix 67

Chapter 7: The Phases of the Dream Pursuit 85

Chapter 8: It Has Nothing to Do With You 107

Chapter 9: It's Bigger than You 119

Chapter 10: A Woman Named Susan 129

Dedication

This book is dedicated to my parents, Bernard and Valerie Horne. The spiritual foundation that was instilled in me, along with the courage to create my life on my own terms, far exceeds any natural inheritance I could ever receive. I honor you and thank you.

Preface

In a world where your validation is based on education, material wealth and acquisitions, societal posturing and social standing, I felt the need to reconnect people to their true selves and purpose. Every person emanates into this world with an assignment unique to them, along with corresponding gifts and attributes that are measured to their destiny. *The Successful Dreamer* is about accepting everything that is the essence of you, while desiring nothing outside of your divine make up. It's about giving yourself permission to be who you uniquely are with no consideration for thoughts and opinions that are not in concert with the revelations you discover concerning your reason for existence, and the corresponding aspirations that are birthed from the realization of purpose.

My desire is that every reader walks away with the courage to unapologetically be themselves, and deliver their gifts to this world without boundaries or limitations. There is unique music that resides in every human being. This music possesses its' own rhythm and cadence that may not coincide with societal norms or standards. The words on these pages are revelation to synchronize your music with your designed conductor, God. When this synchronicity takes place, your audience will appear and be forever impacted by your willingness to adhere your music to its' Creator, and nothing else. There are many realities that exist; only one has the power to give you a healthy perspective in any situation, and deliver outcomes into your life that far exceed your greatest expectations. This reality is God consciousness. Enjoy *The Successful Dreamer* and be postured to unapologetically live your truth.

Chapter 1:

Be Sold On Yourself

"The Authentic You is the best offering you have to deliver to this world."

– Matthew C. Horne

Pieces of other people that you replicate as your own ideas and creations will never compare with the whole divine gift you have to give. The original you is what you showed up here to deliver to this world. This version of you is greater than any other version of anyone that you could ever replicate. To be a successful dreamer, you cannot be anything you want to be, rather, everything you were designed to be. This is about accepting the purpose for your life and the corresponding gifts and talents you've been given to fulfill your purpose, while desiring nothing, in the form of attributes other people may possess.

Every human being was dealt a hand before they showed up here on Earth. Your hand is your gifts, talents, abilities, and attributes along with your unique way and perspective of seeing the world. The moment you embrace your hand, and have no desire to look at anyone else's hand, is when you have set the foundation to become a successful dreamer. The internal conclusive place that you must arrive at is that you can look around and accept that the people to the right and left of you likely have talents and abilities you will never possess, and that you have talents and abilities that are not innate within them. When you have peace with this realization, your focus will go within and you'll understand the attributes you were given that can translate to a life you never imagined.

The Two Dreamers

There are two types of dreamers: Dreamers and successful dreamers. Dreamers concoct whatever outcome they want for their life, based on motive and what society deems as successful. Successful dreamers submit to the calling on their life, with the primary motivation being an understanding that this is the greatest thing they could ever fulfill: a divine calling.

We've seen many people attempt to do things that just weren't in line with their makeup. That "it" factor just wasn't present. It was clear that they didn't have the necessary attributes and innate ability to do what they are trying to convince themselves and others that they can do. Contrarily, we've seen individuals flow so effortlessly in their given talents and arenas that God's divine imprint is the first and only thought that comes to mind.

The universe will speak to you very clearly and consistently until you pay attention to what you are purposed to do with your life. One of the best decisions you can make in life is listening to and adhering to the voice of the universe, whose primary mission is to help you understand what you showed up here to do.

You must go where you feel compelled to go, and do what you feel compelled to do.

Eternity will always speak to you concerning who you are. This voice must resonate above all others if you are to experience life in its' optimal level of fulfillment. This may require you to take what many may deem as significant steps backward away from an established occupation, living situation, or lifestyle. In reality, you've opted for leaps forward toward immeasurable inner prosperity and fulfillment.

Your Blue Print

There are many things you do so effortlessly that they are an unmistakable blueprint to your destiny. Discovering and embracing your blueprint will ensure a life long journey of success. When you are totally focused on what you have to offer and not competing with other people's gifts and talents, you can discover your blueprint.

I can remember being a sophomore in college playing basketball at a Division I school, with my only aspiration being making it to the NBA. I ended up in a speech class, this particular year, and being tasked with giving a persuasive speech as an assignment. The day came to give my speech, and I instinctively gave a speech with the intention of helping my classmates look forward in life and not look back, with this mindset being the cornerstone of success. I had no idea what I had done, given the only reward I wanted for this speech being a grade of an "A" or a "B." When my speech concluded, five of my classmates surrounded me and with the most genuine look in their eyes I had ever seen, said, "You should be a motivational speaker."

It May or May Not Be

The last thing on earth I ever foresaw for my life was being a motivational speaker. When my classmates said this to me, I responded with, "Motivational Speaker?" "I'm six foot-five with a jumper!" "Motivational Speaker?" When I said this, the look in their eyes didn't change. In that moment, I knew their words had credence, and that this was not an ordinary moment. Through a series of events, I was told the exact same thing twice in the next two weeks. After this, I realized that someone had told me this, in so many words, over the summer. At this point, I couldn't run.

Your purpose may be in the realm of something you never imagined for yourself, and that is perfectly fine and normal. Your purpose, when it is revealed and discovered, must be adhered to if you'll ever be a successful dreamer.

Your purpose can be revealed, but has no power until it is embraced.

Be open to what the universe reveals to you about yourself. Accept what you are shown regarding your reason/s for existence. There is an endless amount of provisions and breakthrough's waiting for you if you say "Yes!" to your purpose.

After accepting my calling, I went on to receive my first book contract in my last semester of college at the age of twenty-two. I then went on to write another book as soon as I graduated from college. I was the author of two globally selling books before I was twenty-four years old. Les

Brown, the legendary motivational speaker endorsed my second and third book with testimonials that appear on the book covers. The rest is history, as I've been a successful motivational speaker, author, and entrepreneur for the last fourteen years. This was not stated to glorify my accomplishments, rather to help you gain perspective in regards to choosing your purpose over all other options in creating your life.

I'm saying this to emphasize that you deserve to be sold on yourself, and experience the meteoric rise that comes along with impacting the lives of your fellow man with your gifts and talents. There is only one you, so why not use, your life, to deliver the best offerings you have to give. You showed up here with everything inside you to fulfill whatever you are destined to do.

Society, friends, parents, and family will always have a million different opinions of what you should do with your life.

Finding the courage to be sold on yourself and your innate desires will pay dividends for a lifetime.

Never compare yourself with or compete with your fellow man. If you really want to win in life, continuously become the best version of yourself and incline your ear to the whispers of the universe regarding who you are.

When it comes to undertaking this journey towards everything destiny has for you, remember to be utterly and completely sold on yourself, while giving the universe a resounding yes when your purpose is revealed to you.

The world is waiting for you to give it all of you and no one else.

Notes and Insights

Notes and Insights

Chapter 2:

The Short Account

"Your dreams will materialize when you create the right atmosphere for them to flourish."

-Matthew C. Horne

When you go within yourself and figure out what you really want from life, an uncommon discipline and focus must accompany this. Many people never find something they feel compelled to do with their lives, so finding this is an accomplishment, but is not enough if these desires are ever to materialize. What keeps some dreamers from fulfilling their dreams is the lack of focus and discipline. Being a dreamer is not easy due to everything you have to do to actualize your dreams while going against society's norms and rules. How you move as a dreamer is not congruent with how the majority moves. The successful dreamer must be cognizant of this and always go through life being true to whatever cadence and dance your path requires of you.

I titled this chapter "The Short Account" because there is an overabundance and an ever-present number of factors that will quickly derail you from your primary focus. In order to make it, it is advantageous to not entertain distractions and essentially keep a short account with them by not allowing them to stay in your presence. If you keep an extended account with the wrong things, your primary focus will shift and you'll lose the momentum you were building towards your dreams. This can become dangerous because some dreams and life-aspirations come with a time window. It's better to accept that you must keep a short account with dream deterrents than to have to regain momentum towards whatever dreams you were building.

You Haven't Missed It

There's an all-knowing omniscient Creator behind your existence. You are here for a reason. Even when you veer off your course, there exists the opportunity to realign yourself with whatever dream is for you. The evidence of this is that you are alive and breathing. Every breath you take is with the intention that you will impact the world in only the manner you can. Embrace this gift of life and realign yourself with whatever the universe has revealed to you about who you are, if you got distracted on your journey. Restoration and blessings await you.

There's Power in the Word "No"

Right on cue, when you decide to pursue your dreams and set them in motion, the aforementioned distractions will avail themselves to you. That friend will pop up from out of town. The invites will come when you've designated certain times to further the progression of your dreams. The strongest word in your vocabulary must be "No", as you are developing momentum towards something that could positively change the complexion of your life, for the duration of your years.

At this stage in my career, I show aspiring authors how to write their own books, and through my company, Lightning Fast Book Publishing. My company publishes their books in three weeks, while providing them with a global distribution platform.

One of my most memorable recollections of this is when a prospective author contacted me a week before Christmas in 2016. This client wanted a ghostwriter and to have their book released by Valentine's Day of 2017. I knew this was utterly impossible to do with a ghostwriter, and would require the client to write their own book themselves.

The above-mentioned client was remarkable in that they served in the capacity of a medical doctor. I knew the only way to pull this off was for the client to write the book themselves. This would require extreme dedication from the client given the hours they worked in the hospital, which often required overnight stays in the hospital. In addition, there was a toddler present in this equation on the client's end, upping the level of focus and dedication needed to fulfill such a gargantuan literary task. The client spent every available moment writing their book. The book dealt with female physical empowerment, so it was vital for this book to be done in time for Valentine's Day, which was February 14.

The client wrote their book in three weeks, and with my company, Lightning Fast Book Publishing, we published their book in two weeks. The client had an overabundance of boxes containing printed copies of their book on their doorstep on February 13, 2017. This was made possible by keeping a short account with all external factors that did not accommodate the progression of getting this book done before Valentine's Day.

Isolation

Most people are never going to undertake a dream pursuit, let alone arrive at a place, which represents the ideal definition of success for their life. That is perfectly fine, as different people have varying definitions of fulfillment. No one is wrong in the scheme of dreamers and non-dreamers. Neither dreamers nor non-dreamers are better or worse than the other is. The reality is that these two people move with a different cadence and rhythm through life. There will be times in a dream pursuit where isolation is required due to the way you must move to achieve your dreams, versus how the majority of people move throughout life, and the stark contrast of these ways of existence. You are responsible for creating the necessary atmosphere and environment for creating the things that beckon you to manifest them. I go into more detail on how to create these atmospheres in my book, "All We Have is NOW: How to Create What's Missing and Do It NOW!"

When you truly have clear instructions on what you need to do to create your dreams, you enter into your own energy field. You enter a place of total immersion into the focus and cumulative tasks that must be implemented by you to see your vision to the place of manifestation. This energy field is not congruent with how most people are moving, so a period of natural separation takes place.

If your friends, family, and social acquaintances do not understand your less frequent encounters and interactions with them, your attitude must be, "That has nothing to do with me." There's too much at stake for you to explain yourself. Let me be clear. I encourage you to handle your familial responsibilities and do what you have to do to keep a roof over your head, but there often comes a time when your dream needs everything extra you have to give it; and that is perfectly fine. Everyone should understand that you would be back once your inner vision resides in the realm of tangible reality.

Isolation does not last forever. There just comes a time when your waters are ruffling and you have to go all in. It's just something you know that can't be explained. Every provision and breakthrough resides in this season and space. You have to move with the current of destiny as it pertains to you. You will feel the push from the universe. You will hear its' whispers in your ear. The desire to fulfill this dream will overtake your heart. Give your dream all that you have when this occurs.

Picking Your Spots

Being in my mid-thirties, I often revisit the sacrifices I made in my twenties to set myself for life in my dreams and career as an author. I'm from and reside in the Washington, D.C. area. There was one night when I was twenty-four years old and my friends had invited me out to an establishment in the city. I showed up and stayed for as long as I could. When everyone else was warming up and getting into their rhythm for the night, I was making my departure from the establishment. I had a book signing at the number two-ranked African-American bookstore on the east coast the next morning.

My friends worked their nine to fives all that week. We were young. My friends had every right to enjoy the fruits of their labor. Our cadence was just different given we were on completely opposite paths.

I have no regrets on how I skillfully picked my spots in my twenties, with the outcome being five books that sold globally all before my 30th birthday. This is not an endorsement of myself; it's just the reality of what making sacrifices in your youth can yield you. I lived my twenties and had all the fun I was supposed to. I just knew how to remove myself from the material world when it was time for me to create the various things destiny was impressing upon me. Periodic hibernation will serve you immeasurably. When destiny calls your name, you must answer if you are ever to become a successful dreamer.

Don't Waste Your Twenties

A popular ideology in society is to purely have fun in your twenties and worry about the realities of life in your thirties, as well as how you would like to construct your life moving forward. It's perfectly fine to enjoy your twenties, as you can see that I did in the above chapter. You just don't want to make fun to be everything, while forfeiting the opportunity to focus on your purpose, and begin taking the necessary measures to chart your path towards whatever destiny has in store for you. People may not understand your focus and audacity to undertake something so serious and drastic as living your purpose in your twenties and that is perfectly fine. You were given a lens into your truth, and have the exclusive sight to its power, necessity in the earth, and purpose. Be smart. Pick your spots. Do the things that people in their twenties do, but maximize this period of your life by knowing how and when to separate for the benefit of furthering your calling. The life I live now in my thirties is a direct result of the sacrifices and implementation of focus and persistence that defined my twenties. Set yourself up for life through your choices. You are not too young.

What Calls Your Name?

As a successful dreamer: your main objective has to be your main objective, period. Many things will talk to you in the form of distractions to take your focus away from the type of movements necessary to fulfill your dreams. There will always be an event, an outing, a hangout, or an opportunity for travel, which talks to you while you are exercising laser focus on your dreams. There's nothing wrong with these things talking to you; the problem occurs when these distractions call your name. When your dream calls your name, distractions become faint voices. When dream deterrents call your name, your dream is the faint voice.

Your success as a dreamer hinges on which voice speaks the loudest. I've observed many individuals with great business concepts and ideas that have gotten on their path to fulfilling them. I've also witnessed stagnation and regression while these individuals are still pursuing their dreams. This is due to the wrong things that are not in alignment with their aspirations having the larger portion of these people's ear.

A while ago, I was watching a Magic Johnson documentary. Magic Johnson was the most electrifying basketball player ever to play for the storied Los Angeles NBA franchise. Magic was a part of the Show Time Lakers, which won a total of five NBA championship titles. All of the Hollywood celebrities were courtside in attendance at the games. The Staples Center, which was the Lakers arena, was littered with the who's who of Hollywood elite actors. The style of basketball that Magic Johnson played was Hollywood as well with his no look passes, high octane, and entertaining offense.

This documentary showed Magic poolside at the Hollywood parties as well as other social venues on the Hollywood scene. He was very present in the Hollywood lifestyle, but somehow, as the documentary stated, he continued to improve as a basketball player, evidenced in his elongated championship run with the Lakers. Magic Johnson enjoyed the Hollywood scene as any young, handsome, athletically gifted man would do, but basketball remained his main thing, and called his name above all.

A successful dreamer does not just achieve their dreams and park.

If you are breathing, there's always more that you can create and deposit into your fellow man and the world as a whole.

It is commendable not only to achieve greatness resulting from your efforts; it is remarkable to not get distracted and somehow maintain the focus that landed you into a favorable position in life. Focus is paramount in a dream pursuit, especially in the beginning stages as you fight to establish momentum and results. The next challenge is choosing to listen to that voice giving you that next set of instructions when your bank account, material possessions, and lifestyle do not reflect the early stages of struggle you may have experienced.

As a testament to your Creator who inspired the dreams in you and allowed every corresponding blessing to enter your life, keep the main thing the main thing, even as life rewards you for staying your course. There are more rewards on your path of greatness as you continue to say "yes" to the very things you feel compelled to do. Let your primary motivation be that you are fulfilling what you were put on the earth to do, and consequently your fellow man will be empowered because of this. Always be consumed by your purpose, keeping the world around you and all that it offers in its' proper perspective.

Focus.

Notes and Insights

Notes and Insights

Chapter 3:

Acknowledge or Accept

"Always operate in the realm of reality when pursuing your dreams. The realm of fantasy lends itself to non-substantive results."

-Matthew C. Horne

If you have a goal of losing weight, it's widely known that implementing a healthy diet with consistent exercise will facilitate this desire. Many people, especially during the New Year, flock to gyms with the hopes of an ideal physique. The veteran gym goers often joke about how crowded the gym is after January 1. The sentiment amongst the veterans is that you'll be able to use the gym equipment more easily around March when the new gym crowd goes back to their normal routines, which don't include regular visits to the gym.

Some newcomers stick with it, while others fade quickly with gym visits, being less frequent with every passing week. The one, who sticks with it, ultimately sees the results they desire in their physiques, while the people who choose not to be consistent remain the same physically.

We all know what we must do to achieve our respective dreams. We can easily acknowledge the steps that we must take verbally, but to accept the reality of what we must do is breathing life into that aspiration.

If you accept the reality of what it takes to arrive at your life's desired destinations, you will fully immerse yourself into the steps that you must take, until your dreams are tangible realities.

Dreamers tend to "Know." Successful dreamers tend to "Do."

Fantasy and Allure

The successful dreamer does not undertake a dream pursuit just to impress others. It's very alluring to create something from your gifts and talents and tell people about it so they will view you in a certain light. There are very few people you can reach out and touch who are making a living from living their dreams. The people who live this reality are very alluring, because it takes the characteristics of courage and audacity to arrive at the place of being a successful dreamer. Naturally, people gravitate towards the successful dreamer because; subconsciously they want a piece of whatever attributes and characteristics that empower a particular person to achieve uncommon success on their own terms.

Given this reality, many people undertake a dream pursuit just long enough to convince people that they do a particular thing, with no substance or results to back it up. These people just want the adoration and accolades, while the successful dreamer is usually quiet in their endeavors, because arriving at their destination holds more credence to them than the allure of people thinking they are something special.

The only problem with this is that someone who has weathered their own storms in life and stayed their course towards their dreams, and consequently has become independently successful, will see right through this person. The successful dreamer's results speak for them. The person existing in the realm of fantasy lets their words speak for them.

In my last book, "How to Get Beautiful Women... and Everything Else You Want From Life" I have a chapter titled: "The Success Undershirt." In this chapter, I explain how it's more alluring to a woman if she can peel you back in layers as opposed to you laying your accomplishments at her feet as soon as you meet her, as most men do. In essence, your accomplishments should be worn as an undershirt, as opposed to on your sleeve.

It's more impressive to people when you are very accomplished but don't speak of it. It gives off the impression that you have longevity in your success and that you are comfortable within yourself. If you really want to make an impression on people, actually be who you say you are.

I remember interacting with a young woman when I was in my mid-twenties. I had a couple of books out at the time and a little bit of flash and allure. The young woman, after actually seeing my books, was amazed not at my books, rather with me actually being who I said I was. She wasn't from Washington, D.C. She said that so many men try to impress her with they're "About" to do, and that I was the first person she had met that actually had a tangible result to validate my words.

The irony is that existing in the realm of acknowledgment of what must be done and fantasy, all to impress people, pales in comparison to the impression you'll make on people when in reality you are who you say you are, and have the steady stream of results to validate this.

The Success Frequency

Real results speak at a volume that anyone can interpret without you saying a word. A true successful dreamer does not have to concoct a baseless identity, because your efforts are based in your true nature and calling, accompanied by a diligent focus that takes you to your promised land.

When you have accepted the reality of what it takes to live your dreams, the results will take care of themselves and you won't have to say a word. When you are diligent in the pursuit of your calling and dream, the results will accumulate and be a testament to who you are.

A person who has acknowledged what must be done to live their dreams may actually get some results. However, not to the extent of what they could actually achieve if they accepted the reality of what must be done to live their dreams. That person who goes to the gym for a couple of months may lose a few pounds but they could have lost the thirty or forty pounds they desired if their efforts were based in longevity.

My favorite musician is the rapper Gucci Mane. His lyrics are catchy, but it was his work ethic and results that made me become a fan. Gucci became one of the most recognized names in the music industry by releasing mix tape after mix tape in rapid succession early in his career. He lived in the studio and simply put out more music than anyone else put out. He battled many demons, as many people do, resulting in drug addiction and frequent prison stints. Some prison stints were minor, while others were lengthy. Gucci was always draped in the finest of diamonds and had the lifestyle of a famous rapper, but music was always his main thing. Gucci Mane accepting what he had to do to become a top recognized artist is what propelled him to prominence, even to this day.

Gucci started a record label and began to sign talented artists he knew from the Atlanta, GA area, and beyond. There was one in particular who was catchy named O.J. Da Juice Man. I know. The name is a bit comical. Juice was talented and had many trademark sounds that gravitated people to him and developed a solid fan base. The frequency of his album releases paled into comparison with Gucci Mane's output. Gucci Mane spoke in an interview years ago about how O.J. Da Juiceman had the talent, but the street life called O.J.'s name as opposed to accepting the reality of what must be done to be a successful rapper.

Meaning, O.J. had a little success based off some of his effort, but the success waned because he only acknowledged the effort he needed to put forth, as opposed to accepting it.

The Trappings of Success

Rewards come when you take a consistent approach to the effort and focus necessary to fulfill your dreams. There's nothing like having more notoriety, success and money than you may have experienced ever. All of this is great, but you never want to shift your focus to the rewards and away from what got you the rewards in the first place: Your Gifts and Talents. A fall from grace is seldom followed by a padded landing.

There's absolutely nothing wrong with enjoying the myriad of great things that come with success, as long as they don't take you away from your main thing.

It is a life-mastery skill to be able to maintain the same hunger that propelled you to succeed, when your entire life situation has changed for the better.

The great one's find a way to maintain the level of motivation and focus that propelled them to greatness after they are no longer dreaming, rather living in the reality of the dream.

The successful dreamer understands they'll never arrive until their last breath is taken.

If you are breathing, you have more purpose to fulfill. The universe will continue to whisper the next assignment and endeavor into your spirit. Your existence is meant to be ever evolving.

The Power of Humility

By no stretch of the imagination have I figured it all out when it comes to life and success. I've been in my respective career for a long time and lived every stage of the dream pursuit from struggling to outright prosperity. I often will take time to mentor dreamers and entrepreneurs who are finding their way in the beginning of their journeys. I have a gauge that I base the person's likelihood of actually making it in whatever arena they are pursuing. That gauge is how humble they are, and how they actually handle success.

If a person's demeanor does not change after they experience a little bit of success, meaning they don't become full of themselves, they are likely to go the distance, due to their focus being in the right place. It's the people who feel as if they've accomplished so much, when they've really done nothing at all, who tend not to have the results to match their inflated perception of themselves. I see these people bolster themselves as far as the portrayal of their greatness to others, while having very little in the way of change concerning their real life situations behind the scenes.

Exercising humility will always propel you towards becoming a successful dreamer. You always want to acknowledge your source, your Creator, who gave you the gifts and talents to fulfill the dreams and purpose that were intentionally placed in you.

Let purpose be the guiding light and foreboding thought in your journey to becoming a successful dreamer.

Of all the things that can speak to you, let purpose call your name. With this mindset, you will always accept the realities of what must be done to fulfill your respective endeavors. Never waiver. I've seen many colleagues come and go repeatedly; having to start all over each time, while having lost precious momentum. Stay your course and understand there is a reward, even when things don't look like they will materialize the way you envisioned them. Don't worry about other people's perception of you and the way in which you do things. Exercise humility and know you are living your dreams as a testament to your Creator above all. Accept that significant breakthroughs in life rarely come in the form of a journey that was traveled in a straight line. Accept all realities that come with you living your dreams, and be the remnants of people who actually create the life they envisioned for themselves, through their gifts and talents.

Existing in the realm of fantasy serves you in no way. True substantive abundant living presents itself to you when reality is your gauge, and sustained effort is your way of moving.

Notes and Insights

Notes and Insights

Chapter 4:

The Never Ending Faucet

"Walking in your purpose will ensure a lifetime of prosperity in all facets of life."

-Matthew C. Horne

There are no bounds or limitations to what you can create with your gifts and talents. Opting to be a successful dreamer is to accept the reality that your quality of life is essentially, what you create it to be. This is based on your willingness to have your talents make provision for you. In your dream pursuit, you may find yourself not always getting the monetary outcomes you may have envisioned with the speed and expectation you thought things would materialize, but you must continue moving forward. Keep creating, as your boundless life of prosperity depends on this.

Knowing that you are doing what you were put on earth to do comes with internal peace, regardless of what your situation looks like in any given moment. Even before monetary prosperity finds you, internal prosperity will find you. You will receive signs along the way that you are affecting your fellow man positively as you regularly deliver your gifts and talents to the world. There's an immeasurable satisfaction in knowing you are doing exactly what you were created to do, regardless of the outcomes.

Your purpose existed before you ever showed up here. The greatest satisfaction you can experience in life will be operating in your purpose, resulting from your purpose being at the core of who you are and what you were created to be.

Your purpose will manifest itself in various assignments and inspirations during your lifetime.

That's why we never completely finish or arrive until we no longer have the capacity, physically, to operate in our purpose, due to us taking our last breath.

This is a never-ending faucet because breathing is synonymous with purpose. There's always an assignment to be fulfilled, and always a corresponding reward to your willingness to fulfill your assignments and see them to completion. Never question what you are inspired to do that aligns with your purpose.

Blessings Delivered

The All-Knowing Omniscient Creator, God, gave you your purpose. Since God is all knowing and omniscient, all resources on earth belong to Him. God does not travel in straight lines as the human mind does. We think if we do "x" we will get "y." God can get anything that He wants to you in any given fashion. God rewards efforts, yes. Nevertheless, obedience brings the ultimate rewards. When you have the faith to pursue a dream that there's no tangible evidence of ever materializing, that requires faith in something greater than you. The world's system says, "Do "x" and you will get "y." God's system says do what you're compelled to do. You will get signs and markers along the way to arriving at your destination in life. When you arrive at your destination, you will realize that you've seen this place all along. God's system is all about trusting your instincts. You're never alone. That's why you will receive signs and markers delivered directly from God as you stay the course towards what you are purposed to do.

Some of the most spiritually and financially rewarding blessings I've ever received came from seeming accidents.

In 2012, my mother purchased a table for me to sell my books and advertise my speaking services at an event that she was a part of. I was hesitant to go because my printer was unusually slow in delivering the amount of books I would need for an event like this. I had a new company that I was thinking about starting, which was an expansion of an existing company I had established. Since I only had very few printed books, I showed up to the event with just a laptop computer opened up to my website so people could see and order my books, along with a sign that advertised the new service I had just created. On day two of the event, a woman was in my chair waiting for me as I arrived to the event. She heard about my new services and immediately became my first client.

This service was one of the more prosperous ventures I've undertaken in my years of entrepreneurship. Prosperous in terms of the fulfillment of seeing others be able to live their dreams, in addition to the provisions that enhanced my quality of life.

Stay your course. Blessings can find you from any angle. In 2014, I had an experience that allowed me to see there are seasons for blessings that result from obedience to your calling. The year 2014 was a rough year to say the least, which I'll explain in more detail in chapter seven. I was working out in the gym and a woman approached me and said that she had been trying not to say anything to me, but she felt compelled to do so. She said that it was my time and things would be different for me moving forward, and that God was pleased with me. I don't take encounters like this at face value, because if it's real it will be confirmed through the manifestations in my life that are aligned with those words. Two weeks later, I was conducting a book signing and a woman was witnessing to people at Jesus. She asked to pray with me and I agreed. She also said that it was my time and that God was pleased with me, and that things would not be the same. Not too long after this encounter, I entered a season where my life completely changed, and changed fast. Everything people articulated to me, that they didn't think would happen in my life, happened, and a new level of living and provision became a fixture. I was elevated.

Your efforts are necessary in creating the life you want for yourself, but your obedience to your calling, even when things don't always add up according to what you see, is paramount.

The Power of an Idea

Years ago, I was conversing with a man I knew and explaining what my second book, *The Universe is Inviting You In,* was all about. In the description, I said, "All We Have is NOW." The man looked at me and said, "That's a book title!" There you have it; my third book was set in motion.

There will always be an idea present within you that aligns with your calling that inspires you to create in accordance with what you are purposed to do.

The breakthroughs and blessings you've been fighting for will often manifest themselves in the form of an idea.

Do not take these moments of inspiration lightly, as they have the power to change the complexion of your life forever. You don't know which idea will be the one that catapults you to realms unseen.

Give

I want you to create something of monetary gain from your gifts and talents. I desire that people will show you the value of what you've chosen to deliver to this world, in the form of your gifts and talents. I want you to value yourself enough to place yourself in environments of people who celebrate who you are and what you bring to the table, in the form of your gifts and talents.

This is how you keep the faucet running; you unceasingly give of yourself. Your fellow man is the designed recipient of every gift and talent you possess.

Unimaginable prosperity is available to you when you never stop creating and giving from what has been given to you.

As a professional motivational speaker who sustained in the industry for over a decade; it's safe to say that the words I give to enhance people's lives are substantive and more impactful than normal conversations about life. This is not to glory in myself. This is an acknowledgment to the power and impact of the gift I was given. My conversation is valuable. Even though I am a paid professional speaker, I still take time to make deposits into people's lives, through guiding conversations, when I feel compelled to do so. I give back through mentorship. I don't always get a return in the moment, but that is fine because I know the return is on its way. I'd prefer a return from the All-Knowing Omniscient Creator than anything of momentary value a particular person could have offered me in a given moment. Giving is never in vain, and the return can overtake you in a boundless fashion.

When you give of yourself, there are times when people will not keep their word, and uphold their end of an agreement. There are times where people will blatantly and skillfully be conniving toward you. It's ok. Your Creator sees it all. When you are stress free, drama free, debt free and can have anything you want and go anywhere you'd like to go, remember this is a bi-product of not just your obedience to your calling. In addition, the deposits that you've willingly made into for others through your gifts, always comes back. You're a human being. You will possibly feel frustration and anger in moments where people blatantly take advantage of you. In these moments, acknowledge your Source. Acknowledge that you were obedient with the gifts you were given, and that a boundless blessing is eminent, given the scope of your Creator. It always comes back.

Notes and Insights

Notes and Insights

Chapter 5:

The Financial Lifestyle of the Dreamer

"Having no debt facilitates endless creativity while loosening the financial vice that suffocates dreams."

-Matthew C. Horne

The beauty about living your dreams is that your finances cannot be regulated. There's no cap on your income. You can have consecutive months where your income supersedes a yearly corporate salary. I'm talking about the type of money that makes you unemployable. It's an unrivaled feeling to wake up every morning when you are finished sleeping, and can do whatever you'd like to do with your day. This is made possible by having the money to do that comfortably.

There is financial prosperity in being a successful dreamer. You're giving your best to the world, and consequently getting the best in return. There's beauty in massive financial gains from your gifts. There's more satisfaction in actually keeping your money and maintaining the lifestyle, your money has created for you. I've seen many people become massively wealthy living their dreams, only to dig themselves into financial holes that are insurmountable, with the fault being their own. I've seen the loss of houses, businesses, assets and much more due to poor financial management.

This is a very important chapter given that being a wise financial steward over your money can change your life, and set the stage for generations to come. Money is a powerful tool that must be respected. There are simple lifestyle choices and changes that will ensure that you can comfortably live your dreams without adding the financial pressure to your equation, bearing unnecessary stress on you and those around you.

I can remember watching ESPN's 30 for 30 series titled: "Broke." This documentary chronicled the financial ruin of many multimillion-dollar athletes. At the core of the failure of these athletes was that they earned life-changing sums of money very quickly, but never took the time to understand money. The bible states, "A fool and his money are soon parted." A fool is someone who willingly remains ignorant. There's an education about money available to anyone. A great place to start is Dave Ramsey's practical financial wisdom and programs. I implore you to value the power of money, especially when you see massive gains from your dream pursuit. Educate yourself on how to keep it. The power is in the retention and growth of your money. In the documentary, the main culprit to the loss of wealth were groupies, undue financial pressures from family and friends, bad investments, terrible spending habits, with the financial undertaker being these athlete's own financial advisors. Of the many culprits these athletes who were interviewed spoke of, it was mainly the people who they were supposed to be able to trust, their financial advisors, who fleeced them clean.

In general, whether you are wealthy or make a respectable living, it's great to develop a healthy and progressive relationship with money. As a successful dreamer, your name will be made great, due to the notoriety of effectively using your gifts to help others and the corresponding increased public profile. People are coming for your money. Make sure your businesses are legit and you are protected from loss. Vet the individuals who attempt to enter your atmosphere, as motives will play out, good and bad, over time. Keep a consistent and vigilant eye on your money.

When it came to the documentary "Broke," what perplexed me the most was people's willingness to just hand over their hard earned millions to financial advisors and not keep an eye on it. These money managers were outright stealing money from these athletes, using the athlete's money to fund personal investments by using fake withdrawal signatures. These financial advisors were running wild financially on these athletes, with no repercussions, many times after the fraud was exposed. The scariest part was that many of these fraudulent financial advisors were approved by the NFL and NBA. The bottom line is if people know you have real money, they're coming for it. Learn how money works, so your money can provide you the unimaginable lifestyle that you deserve. Take personal responsibility for acquiring and maintaining your financial means. When it comes down to it, trust no one more than you trust yourself with your money.

It seems to be a daily occurrence to hear about the latest athlete or entertainer, who has been fleeced. It's logical to believe that multimillionaire dreamers would keep an airtight view of their finances after seeing so many of their counterparts lose it all, due to poor decision-making. I understand the power of money and have a healthy respect for it because I remember not having much of it. I want you to experience the freedom of having real money that you can touch, which can buffer any sudden financial misfortune. I want you to have that air about you that exudes no stress in the face of a wide spread financial crisis. This life is available to any person willing to explore the best they have to offer to this world in the form of their gifts and talents. You can plot your way out of the matrix with high earning habits and great money management. Respect and understand the power of money, and you will possess every provision you need with no worries.

Live Below Your Means

Living below your means is not encouraged in society. There's always something being advertised to you that is "so much more glamorous" than what you already have. According to Gobankingrates, 58 percent of Americans have less than $1,000.00 amassed in savings. Many Americans are in this financial predicament by choice. Many people have made tremendous amounts of money over time, only to sleep walk financially through frivolous and mindless spending habits over time.

Living below your means sets the stage for you to always be able to save money. Being comfortable in your own skin is the cornerstone of living below your means. If you do away with the need to compete with others, keep up with everyone on social media, and engage in reckless and non-disciplined spending, you can create a sizable financial reserve. Living below your means really serves you when you begin to become prosperous in your monetary earnings.

When you have a tremendous amount of money coming in, coupled with the discipline not to change your lifestyle, you will have a financial umbrella on any rainy day.

A strong financial reserve is paramount to your ability to become and sustain your ability to be a successful dreamer.

Stress-free living fuels creativity. Imagine how much you could explore your creative depths if you didn't have the burden of a low bank account and mounting debts. Money is directly correlated to the freedom to move about through life as you please. A sizable amount of money saved can save you in slow periods of business, as you have enough money to sustain you while you plot and execute your next venture. Money truly does answer all things.

Pay Cash for It

You heard it right; pay cash for it! Paying cash for all of your possessions sounds outlandish, as the governing monetary philosophy of the world says to finance whatever you want, live beyond your means and worry about the rest later. When you live below your means, a strange thing happens; you actually can access large sums of money when needed. Stay with me please. This can be you. I promise. At one stage of my dream pursuit, I had overdrawn bank accounts. As I stayed my course, I was able to pay cash for vehicles and anything else I wanted.

Having every possession, large and small, paid for in cash gives you the freedom to wake up with no debt. Waking up with no debt leads to an abundance of creative ideas, and your life becomes a blank canvas that you can decorate into whatever fashionable life suits you. Even if you currently have debt, this is a life-changing habit that can get you on the road to becoming debt-free.

Having the mindset of, "If I can't pay cash for it, I can't afford it," keeps you from the grips of debt that has enthralled the lives of millions of Americans. When it comes to financing the necessary variables that you need to fulfill your dreams, stay disciplined and buy everything with your own money. Be smart. Be resourceful. When you invest in your own dreams, every return comes back to you, without compromise. I remember the days, early in my career, when I literally wasn't buying any new clothes. I was publishing my books solely with my money. I was taking the profits from my sales and re-investing them into my business, until I had everything necessary to build the platform I needed to be a viable public figure and proceed with my career at the level that befitted me.

I had the excuse of being young and blowing money if I chose to, but I chose my calling and the dreams that God placed in my heart.

You can gamble on anything in this lifetime; you are your best option.

Financial Cycles

Life is cyclical. Everything and everyone goes through seasons. To become and remain a successful dreamer you need a sizeable amount of money that you can touch when you need it. You will be up financially and down other times. How you prepare financially determines if the down times are a setback, or an opportunity to comfortably create your way into a better financial situation.

I have witnessed many people who were winning financially for years lose it all due to thinking the financial windfall would last forever. They financed possessions when they could have paid cash. They acquired unnecessary possessions as status symbols, only to give it all back when business to a turn. The reversals of financial fortune could have easily have been navigated, without disruptions in lifestyle, if these individuals would have planned accordingly. Some of these individuals took losses that may be insurmountable, with their lifestyles being changed forever.

You don't have to be completely rigid financially. It's ok to enjoy life within your means, which are comfortable for you. My family squeezes a vacation out of me from time to time. My mother is fancy, so she gets only the best restaurants on my watch. I'm an advocate of being honest with yourself in relation to your finances. If you take this approach, and understand that it's great to even go without things that you can pay cash for and can afford, you'll be completely ahead of the pack financially, and have the corresponding freedom and peace that comes along with no financial stresses.

There Are No Guarantees

In Washington, D.C., it is widely known that a government job is the most secure form of employment a person can have. We recently received a reminder that nothing is secure when it comes to finances; this reminder came in the form of an elongated government shut down. Many people were without paychecks for a lengthy period. Many people's lives were unexpectedly altered as a result of losing a couple of paychecks.

I do not want to appear insensitive, but many of these people's lives did not have to be turned upside down financially. Their reserve fund that could have made this period a momentary light affliction, was eaten away with fine dining, vacationed on exotic getaways, driven away in automobiles that are to the letter of their income. Rainy days are inevitable. Your attitude towards money and corresponding consistent money habits will determine the severity of life's financial storms when they arrive at your doorstep.

Entrepreneurship is Non-Negotiable

Not everyone is purposed to be a full-fledged entrepreneur. I get it. This life is for the people who it is for. Given the aforementioned example of the government shutdown, it is evident that it is financially dangerous to rely solely on a job that someone gave you. This is voluntary vulnerability, given that a person can dictate how and when you are paid.

We all have the ability to create something of monetary gain from our gifts and talents. Given the hand you were dealt, that is up to you to determine. This should be worked simultaneously with your job. If the job disappears for whatever reason, you will still have income that you control. Your gifts literally have the power to create provisions for you in any financial climate.

During the recent government shutdown, there were individuals who were out of work, and may not have had any money saved, but were still able to stay afloat due to their additional revenue stream from their business. There is no excuse. Monetize your gifts and talents even if full-fledged entrepreneurship is not your lot it life. I was enthralled to see so many individuals turn inward during the recent government shutdown. They recognized that there were vulnerabilities in the most secure job on earth, and undertook entrepreneurial endeavors, immediately. Entrepreneurship is a powerful avenue to explore, when and before your back is against the wall financially.

Have a Product

Whether you are a full time employee or an entrepreneur, you always want to have a product. You need something that you can sell hand to hand without meetings being set up along with other red tape. I'm writing this book, right now, to enhance your life and for you to be sold on yourself and the endless possibilities of your gifts and talents. That is one reality. This book is also a product. All of my books are products. If a financial downturn came across my path, I would have books in hand, knowing that I could enhance the lives of other people, and consequently, make financial provisions for myself as well. I can remember being in the barbershops and train stations selling my books early in my career. Have the necessary hunger to sell your product and you can dictate your desired climate in any financial forecast.

Make it a Lifestyle

It's beneficial to create a healthy and disciplined relationship with money.

Having above adequate amounts of money means that you can style your life however you'd like to. Not having enough money means that your life will be styled for you.

I wrote this chapter because I understand that this lifestyle of financial freedom is available to you. Living your truth and delivering your absolute best to the world accommodates an unquantifiable return. Gamble on your gifts and talents, without ceasing, and you will have an all-inclusive stay in your promised land. The no-debt lifestyle is waiting for you. Houses and vehicles being paid off are waiting for you. The eradication of major debts such as student loans and credit cards is waiting for you. With a true inventory of your gifts, talents, abilities, and the willingness to create something impactful from your findings, you can create a life where the worldly rules of survival do not apply to you, while you operate outside of the confines of the matrix and the systems in place to engineer our existence and control us.

The Best Investment

In the pursuit of your dreams, there will be many opportunities from others that people present to you, due to your qualities of courage and audacity, exemplified in your dream pursuit. There are many opportunities to "invest" in that will befall you. My thought processes on some of these investments is simply looking at the return that I am receiving financially in life as a successful dreamer. Often, the conclusion I make is that my money is better served in my possession, given that it gives me the cushion, peace, and freedom to continue to pursue my dreams. Often times whatever return I may or may not receive at the end of this proposed investment pales in comparison to what I could easily generate in a matter of weeks or months.

Understand, while you are still finding your way as a dreamer how powerful your dollar is as it relates to the ability to continue to pursue your dreams. You always want to remain on solid financial footing so that distractions are minimal as you move towards your promised land. Debt and poor financial management is the current of the world, and by design. The intention of the population moving this way is that they remain vulnerable and easily susceptible to being controlled. Your money is your escape from this governing paradigm. I present to you, "How to Escape the Matrix"...

Notes and Insights

Notes and Insights

CHAPTER 6:

How to Escape the Matrix

"When your eyes are opened you'll see some things that cannot be unseen. Pay homage to these revelations and never move the same way again."

-Matthew C. Horne

The God in you is greater than the matrix. Your purpose supersedes the boundaries of systematic engineering and controlled confines for segments of the population. You were created to exceed any boundary or limitation that could ever be imposed upon you. You are infinite. You are limitless. Your origin is eternal, from a place where time, space, and confines are non-existent. You are greater than the built-in checks and balances that you will encounter when you dare to venture in the opposite direction of the popular current and culture. You are unstoppable.

The matrix is the systematic control and boundaries that are established for the population to forward the agenda of those who have so much power, through wealth, that they would never allow others to reach their pinnacles of success. The matrix controls school curriculums so that financial astuteness is never established, training every person to be ignorant to the power of money and wealth, while never encouraging out of the box thinking that would empower you to the point that you create your life, your way, with confines being the furthest reality you will encounter. The matrix is rooted in control and ignorance to its schemes and existence. The matrix thrives on your identity being outside of you, and whoever you are purposed to be from the All Knowing Omniscient Creator.

In my opinion, this is the construct of the matrix.

Student Loan Debt

Education is the cornerstone of success in the foreboding mantra. You must get a bachelor's degree to become gainfully employed in this society. With this degree you must fight and plow to gain employment, with the loans for this illustrious education being due moments after you cross the graduation stage. You will likely repay the loan on this $100,000.00 education for the rest of your life, and will end up costing the debtor close to $200,000.00 when it is finally repaid. This is the entryway to financial slavery and control over your finances.

The irony in this is that many billionaires such as Bill Gates and Mark Zuckerburg dropped out of their prestigious universities because they could see their dreams were only confined by traditional education. The return on their ideas far exceeded the returns their collegiate education could garner them. Two billionaires we can see with our own eyes saw something so detrimental to their potential that they parted ways with it. What did they see?

With low and stagnant wages being the norm. The constant threat of a weak economy, many people are opting for untraditional means of making a living that don't require a higher education. Professions such as trades and public services are being considered by many in the face of realizing that traditional education is making less and less sense with every passing year.

To make matters worse there exists an insane competition for high paying jobs. Usually these jobs require Post-Graduate degrees, which equates to acquiring hundreds of thousands of dollars of more debt.

I'm an advocate of education. I believe a person should get a degree in something that has the earning potential to eradicate the accompanying student loans. I'm also in tune with reality. Figuring out your purpose early on and getting a head start in it by not going to college is a viable and intelligent option in terms of framing your life in such a way that the confines of debt have no power over you.

Car Loans

After you get the degree, the matrix says you have to prove to the world how successful you are. That status symbol vehicle now calls your name, and your automobile from college which is less attractive, and may not measure up to someone with your level of education, must be done away with and replaced. In walks the car note.

A cornerstone of the matrix is proving your value to others through the acquisition of meaningless material possessions.

This is more interest accruing debt that is now in tandem with your student loan debt.

Clothing

Your Instagram has to pop! You are an educated elite and the world must be able to see this all over you in the form of your appearance. The latest designer trends must be a fixture in your closet. The television and entertainment stars who perpetuate and uphold the fashion standards have a closet that yours must rival. They are paid by the designers to wear these fashions, while you pay for them. They're multimillionaires! You are finding your way in the world, yet your fashion must assimilate to the latest and most expensive trends. The clothing validates you, as a mover and shaker in the eyes of people you encounter and is the mantra of the matrix. Stay designer down, at whatever expense. Put it on a credit card. No one must out do you.

Vacations

There is nothing wrong with vacations if you can afford them. No issue exists with anything presented in this chapter if you can comfortably afford them. The problem is that many people can't and they voluntarily place themselves in life long financial constraints with every flight and selfie.

With your higher education degree, matching vehicle, and designer wardrobe you must travel the world. All of societies' and social media's darlings post pictures in their designer threads in the most exotic of places. Nothing separates you from them, and those closest to you and beyond must understand. The matrix says get on that payment plan to secure the priceless Instagram pictures. That's it. Flex on everybody who comes within eyeshot of your timeline. Those double taps and likes have you feeling like a celebrity. Those comments of adoration under your exotic photos show you that your investments have not been in vain. Your self-esteem is now fueled by the drug of validation. The matrix has its' hooks in you. You don't have the money... no problem. Do what you always do when you want something; charge it!

Credit Cards

By now you're beginning to see more month left after the end of your money. The student loans, car payments, fancy dinners, vacations, wardrobe, and so on dissolve your paycheck before it even hits your hand. The show must go on in spite of this. You have a captive audience. The financial gaps must be bridged somehow. Enter the credit card.

A clear indicator that it's probably not a good idea to purchase something is if you have to go into debt to acquire it.

Credit card debt is collectively astronomical, fueled by a population infatuated with living beyond their means. The agenda of the matrix is forwarded as the population goes deeper into debt, with their primary focus being staying on top of their debts, with no thought of entertaining their dreams and purpose, which could create a debt-free life without any sort of confines.

You have to have credit, says the matrix. Accumulate your credit cards. The better credit you have the more value that you have in society, says the matrix. Credit is paramount in your ability to borrow money and incur debt. Please pay attention to the tactics of the matrix that are right in front of your face. So, your value in society is based on how much debt you can potentially accumulate? Think about that. That woman or man says I won't marry them unless they have good credit. I won't marry them unless I know we can maximize our ability to incur more debt over our lifetime. The matrix is wicked.

False Bench Marks of Success

This is where the matrix has many people fooled; $100,000.00 a year is real money. If you are financially wise, this salary is a blessing that you could use to maneuver your way to lasting financial freedom through saving and smart investments. The issue is that the aforementioned matrix tools of destruction are a fixture in the life of the majority of the population.

Let's say an individual takes home five to six thousand dollars a month after taxes. You have the student loans, car note, mortgage/rent, credit card debt and other luxuries and expenses. That money is gone, or close to being spoken for, before it hits your hand. The message that the matrix perpetuates is that you can deem yourself at the upper echelon of society if you make six figures. That was what all the fight was for with education being sold to us as the avenue to success. The matrix understands the amount of money that had to be invested to acquire the six-figure salary. The matrix wins. In essence, the individual who makes $40,000.00 a year is sitting in the same rush hour traffic as the individual who makes $140,000.00 a year. They are both fighting to maintain their possessions, with the only difference being that the individual who makes $140,000.00 a year has shinier toys.

How Do You Escape The Matrix?

You simply do not let society impose a definition of success upon you. You develop a healthy relationship with yourself so that you are at one with yourself no matter where you scale in the tiers of society. You walk through life with nothing to prove, understanding that your breakthroughs may or may not be on par with society's schedule of success. If you are comfortable in your own skin, the matrix has no power over you and cannot usher you to places on the dance floor that make you susceptible to its agenda to control every aspect of your life.

If you have nothing to prove, you will operate outside of the devices of the matrix.

If your identity is not in the material world and societal definitions and benchmarks, you'll always be true to yourself.

You'll be more apt to live below your means and have the financial means to make power moves when destiny calls your name through inspiration to be who you truly are.

The matrix is predicated on keeping you broke no matter how much money you make. There are jobs that elite classes of people want no parts of. There are positions of power and wealth that the mega wealthy societies never want common people to be able to infiltrate. If you can be indoctrinated into a financial system that never was designed for you to win, and continue to place your identity in whatever money draining material possession the matrix says will validate you in society, then you are a pawn in their agenda.

A working class of people is necessary to uphold the matrix. The worst type of employee is an employee with significant amounts of money in the bank. This worker cannot be controlled and manipulated. If there are too many employees that have too much money saved up then that is a direct threat to the workforce that supports the matrix.

    I can't count how many times new management comes into a job, with their people and pushes everyone out of the company. They begin with documentation of disciplinary action against you until they feel you can safely be terminated with no legal ramifications. I've seen this with friends, family members and beyond. It happens so much that many just choose to resign when the "fix" was put into play because they've experienced this so much. However, what about the employee who has hundreds of thousands of dollars in the bank, and management begins to place the sabotage in motion to get them terminated? This employee will likely take time to evaluate their life, and possibly conclude that they never want to be in this vulnerable of a position ever again. The former employee who is unemployed with no stress wakes up every day enjoying the freedoms of life that were so foreign over the years. This employee then decides they are going to start a business, given they have years' worth of money saved up. This business eventually flourishes, with paydays coming in a week that far outweighed their yearly corporate salary. This former employee is now unemployable to the corporate world because corporate money no longer makes sense. The matrix has lost a member of the work force which supports its' very existence.

This example is the very reason the matrix does not want you financially empowered. This is why money management is not a fixture in education as it should be. The less money you have, the more vulnerable you are. The cyclical nature of life means you'll be in situations that are financially favorable and unfavorable. You have to prepare yourself for these times, because they are not a respecter of persons.

The Perpetual Dangling Carrot

The matrix can be simplified to a perpetual dangling carrot. Just when you think you acquired the necessary education, social standing, and material possessions you find out there's more. When you acquire the next hot thing, you find out there's something else. This is the matrix. The powers keep you entangled in this web by always rolling out something new that will validate you and your social standing in society.

A few years ago, I took my vehicle into the Mercedes-Benz service center for repairs. They, in turn, gave me a loaner vehicle with awe striking features. In my possession, temporarily, was a GLE truck that was so technologically advanced you could only laugh in amazement at some of the features. At night, when you opened the driver and passenger side door the Mercedes-Benz logo lit up on the ground like the bat signal. I lost it momentarily when I saw this. I couldn't believe what I was seeing.

If I wasn't fully aware of the tactics that were being implemented by the dealer, I may have been susceptible to purchase the vehicle. My vehicle was perfectly fine and was mine free and clear, so I came back to reality quick after seeing this amazing technology. What about the person who dropped their vehicle off as I did, received the same GLE truck, but had a different reaction? Suppose they had the 2014 instead of the 2016 model. What if the 2014 had the exact same technology as the 2016, minus the Mercedes-Benz logo? Many people would have forfeited their existing payments they already made on their current vehicle, and picked up an entirely new debt for the 2016 truck. This is the matrix.

I promise you the technology of the lit logo hitting the ground existed likely a decade or more earlier than when Mercedes actually rolled out the technology. That's what the matrix is. It's never enough, and they know how to keep you engaged.

The men who set me up with the loaner vehicle told me that since I had a certain class of Mercedes-Benz their intention was for me to fall in love with the truck so I would purchase it. I'm not making this up. He told me how successful this "loaner" strategy was in general. The perpetual dangling carrot nature of the matrix is real.

The Town Hall Meeting

Years ago, when former President Barack Obama was running for re-election he participated in a LinkedIn town hall meeting where the theme was "Putting America Back to Work." President Obama heard the attendees concerns about the economy, which were mostly worrisome given the economy was in an undesirable condition, while joblessness was an eminent reality in America. One by one, the people asked President Obama about the safety of their retirement funds, social security possibly being non-existent, programs for retired military veterans obtaining employment, and legislation for non-discriminatory hiring practices. These questions came from people who were fearful about the detriments of the current state of the economy and how it directly affected them and their loved ones.

There was one man, however, whose dialogue differed drastically from everyone else's. As he addressed the President, he explained that he was unemployed by choice. This gentlemen stated that he was a part of a start up in Silicon Valley, California that went on to do very well, and quite frankly he became independently wealthy as a result of his involvement in this startup company. President Obama and everyone else in attendance knew which startup he was referring, so President Obama humored everyone by asking what kind of startup this was. The man, in his modesty, said it was a search engine. The man was involved with Google and became extremely wealthy. He asked President Obama to raise his taxes to empower the majority of American citizens financially, the same Americans who were by his side on this day raising their concerns about the economy and joblessness.

President Obama paused, and it was as if the spirit hit him, and he said in response to this man, "America's success is premised on individuals and entrepreneurs having a great idea; going out there and pursuing their dreams and making a whole lot of money in the process. And that's great. That's part of what makes America so successful."

President Obama also previously stated that he had solutions that were beneficial to the American people, but the opposing parties were more concerned with making him look bad as a president, than they were with bettering the condition of the American people. In so many words, my deduction of the president's statement was this: The economy is in a mess. I'm trying to fix it against much opposition. Go out there and find the passions that are unique to you. Go out there and pursue your dreams, and make a whole lot of money in the process. In essence, you should go against this matrix that is failing you. Become so wealthy that when the economy resets itself and snatches the rug from under middle class America, you, too, can be like this man, in the financial driver's seat, unfazed by collective economic crisis, in a position to offer solutions during financially dire times, as opposed to being negatively affected by them.

The President gave us an escape from the matrix. The limitless nature of pursuing your dreams is the avenue to prosperity in any given economic climate.

Take Dominion

I am just the messenger when I say this: If a possession can wake you up and make you do anything that you would not like to do, rather have to do, to maintain it, that possession has dominion over you. The real escape from the matrix is when all of your material possessions are paid in full. If you are in an economically dire position or an economically prosperous position, your lifestyle remains the same. This way of living is the complete opposite of what we're told is possible. It directly clashes with the theory of "credit" and "financing" ruling everything. It is the indoctrination of the matrix, which keeps countless people susceptible to its agenda and tactics. You have an overabundance of gifts and talents that were given to you, with the intention that you will be in a favorable financial situation in any climate. Now go out there and pursue your dreams, and make a whole lot of money in the process.

Notes and Insights

Notes and Insights

Chapter 7:

The Phases of the Dream Pursuit

"Accept the cadence and rhythm of your dream pursuit even if it does not align with society's tune."

-Matthew C. Horne

I have been blessed to see my dream pursuit see the beginnings of suspense and hope, to a solid foundation that has borne, and will bear fruit for years to come. I have also observed the dream pursuit of other successful dreamers, and in doing so quantified some patterns that dreamers often go through on their way to achieving their respective breakthroughs.

The three phases of the dream pursuit are as follows:

1. Faith and Humility
2. Separation
3. Accumulation

Faith and Humility

There is no straight line in a dream pursuit. Some people experience breakthroughs and prosperity faster thanothers do in the scheme of dreamers and their pursuits. Faith and humility are paramount qualities to a successful dreamer. Your dream pursuit may not yield the streamlined results of individuals who chose not to live their dreams, rather to make a living. This is okay. As a successful dreamer, you will have to be content if other people accumulate material possessions faster and sooner than you do. It may seem as if people around you are reaching societal benchmarks of success rapidly, and you are behind in the accumulation of the tokens of success. This is where the need for faith and humility enters the equation. You need faith that you will reach your breakthroughs in life even when natural indicators may not support this belief. You'll need humility so your perception of yourself does not change as others accumulate possessions in accordance with society's timelines. Humility will allow you to celebrate everyone around you as they do "better" than you do in certain moments.

Humility will allow you to be comfortable in your own skin, even when others are critical of you and the audacity that you possess, with the belief that you can actually live life in a way that is rare in society.

The dreamer will be criticized, especially when they are not reaching societal benchmarks on the world's schedule.

This criticism will be both open and closed. Your sense of self, meaning that your definition of who you are is in line with who your Creator says you are. This has to be at the core of your being to fuel your dream pursuit in spite of both subtle and vicious opposition.

You are putting your time, energy, effort, and resources into your dream. I hope that you have an expectation and desire for a reward from giving the best of yourself to this world. There's no salary when you completely go out on your own to pursue your dreams. This where faith has to be present; present in the fashion of you trusting that the All Knowing Omniscient Creator who placed the dream inside of you will honor your efforts of diligently doing the work you were created to do. In a world where we're told to get an education and a good job, faith has to be your constant companion, as you make a daring attempt to create a life of success against the world's system.

Grow Your Audacity

Audacity causes your ambition to grow legs.

To think that you can create a life of success outside of the matrix and social engineering takes audacity. This character trait will carry you to your various finish lines in life. The opposition will be real, but audacity will make the efforts of critics futile.

Many people want to pursue their dreams. We all emanate from the same source of Creation. Purpose and destiny speaks to us all. Envy surfaces in the form of people who don't have the audacity to pursue the various things in life that they know are for them. People don't necessarily know if you'll make it or not, but the courage to actually do what your heart is telling you to do with your life is offensive to some, because they don't possesses the traits of courage and audacity.

Many of these dream detractors criticize you, while simultaneously admiring you. There's not much logic in this paradigm because people are complex and multifaceted. Some of the people who were the most critical of me came for my assistance in pursuing their dreams when they saw my dreams were tangible realities. Unbelievably, you will be the breakthrough in the life of some of your greatest detractors, given they witnessed your journey to success, and now feel empowered to pursue their own passions in life. Don't take any of the detractors and their tactics personally. Their attempts to stop you from pursuing your dreams are often rooted in their own insecurities. Be the light you were designed to be to all who you encounter.

Let faith be your guiding light in every weather condition in route to your promised land.

Separation

There is a period of separation from others, and the foreboding indoctrination of this world, that is inevitable in a dream pursuit, given you are moving in the opposite current of society and its' norms. This period of separation will indoctrinate you with the norms and realities of what it takes to actually live your dreams. You will physically be in many of the same places; the world will just begin to look different to you. The reality of what it actually takes to live your dreams and thrive will become apparent with every passing day of your dream pursuit. As this happens you will adapt and the totality of you will begin to posture itself to what must be done to accommodate the realization of your dreams.

There Are Witnesses Around You

It's great to identify people around you who are living their dreams. The universe will hand deliver people and experiences to you to aid in your arrival to your promised land. When I was twenty-two years old, I went to New York to see a speaker who had offered me my first book contract. Upon waiting on the arrival of the speaker and young woman who was also there to see the speaker that day, and I struck up a conversation. I let her know that I had just signed my first book contract and am taking a head first plunge into the self-development industry. I was literally days removed from graduating from college and I was all in. The young woman who was maybe in her thirties or early forties felt my energy, and observed the commonalities of a love of self-development. This young woman had a ticket, free and clear, to attend a four-day Tony Robbins seminar in Denver, Colorado. She said that she had many friends who were business owners who could be enriched by attending such an event, but none of them wanted to go, to her surprise. She concluded that maybe I was the destined recipient of her ticket. Tony Robbins was and is the top motivational speaker in the free world.

The young woman contacted me less than a week after we met and informed me that her friends still didn't want the ticket, and that it was mine. I booked a flight to and hotel in Denver and was at the feet of the top motivational speaker in the world days after graduating from college.

Looking back, I believe that I was positioned there to let me know that I made the right decision to pursue my dream of becoming a motivational speaker and author directly out of college. The words that were coming out of the top motivational speaker's mouth at this conference were my natural thought processes. With every passing moment, as I was in attendance, I knew this industry was for me, in spite of the many people challenging my age and life experiences.

Your purpose operates completely outside of rules, regulations, time, and space.

You have an eternal purpose. All of eternity will align itself with you and your dream pursuit because you said "yes," and exercised faith through a continued and concerted effort towards fulfilling your calling.

The Alignments

The alignments were happening quickly after I graduated from college. The days at the Tony Robbins conference were very long. We got periodic breaks. On one of my breaks, I went back to my hotel room and turned on the television. Dr. Wayne Dyer, a motivational speaker, came on the public access television and he was promoting his new book, *Inspiration: Your Ultimate Calling*. Dr. Dyer said many things that captivated and intrigued me in his time on the screen, but what stuck with me the most was his description of how he wrote his book. Dr. Dyer said that spirit would wake him up precisely at the same time every morning, and the words for his book would come from "no where to now here". He essentially said that the spirit was writing a book through him. He didn't have to set an alarm clock, and many of the words in his book were revealed to him as he wrote. This was amazing, and in no way a coincidence.

After the conference was over, I boarded my flight from Denver, Colorado and was headed back home to Baltimore Washington International Airport. On this flight, my intention was to sleep, given the rigorous days of motivation and inspiration that was the Tony Robins conference. Something was being birthed in me. I couldn't sleep and a book was calling me to write it. My first book contract was for a co-authored project. I outlined my first solo book, *The Universe Is Inviting You In* on this flight back home. The title and corresponding chapters just came to me. I had a solid outline by the time the airplane landed. I proceeded to write the first three chapters in three days following my arrival back home.

The opposition was immediate as I faced it in my own household and from spiritual leaders I respected and admired. I didn't see it coming, but this is what dreams are made of. I was told everything from, "My stomach cringes every time you talk about that book," to "No one is going to buy your book."

God is so amazing and all knowing that He goes before you. A woman in my church purchased Dr. Wayne Dyer's new book, *Inspiration: Your Ultimate Calling,* on audio unexpectedly, and through divine inspiration this woman gave the audio book to my mother, who was not into this type of material at the time. My mother, in turn, gave it to me.

The opposition only intensified and never seemed to relent, but the attempts to deter me from writing my book affected me in no way. I listened to Dr. Dyer's book every morning as I fixed my pancakes. It was routine. The message in his book was to give yourself permission to be whatever you were uniquely created to be. He emphasized that there would be well-meaning people who will attempt to thwart your efforts towards fulfilling your purpose, but to just dismiss them and stay fixated on what you are inspired to do. Dr. Dyer was all about in-spirit consciousness and not letting anyone deter you from whatever you feel compelled to do. He explained, through examples, how the right assistance would materialize precisely when you need it, when it comes to fulfilling your purpose in life, if you've made the choice to participate actively in creating the visions you see from within. Ironically enough, Dr. Wayne Dyer was my assistance precisely when I needed it. His doctrine was my mantra as I sidestepped every attempt to halt my pursuit of my life's purpose.

I Honor You

I'd like to take this portion of my book to honor the memory and impact that the late Dr. Wayne Dyer had on countless people individuals during his time on this planet. I am forever thankful for encountering Dr. Wayne Dyer, and understand that coincidence was nowhere in the equation of having crossed paths with his doctrine. Rest in paradise Dr., Wayne Dyer... Namaste.

You Are Not Alone

You are never alone when you submit to your calling and pursue whatever is for you in this lifetime. You will receive the assistance you need, precisely when you need it. Your Creator is all knowing and omniscient, so He knows what you need and what you will encounter, and has already set the provisions up in your favor, to facilitate the arrival to your life's destinations. At times, you may feel alone; as there are very few people you can reach out to and touch who are making a living, living their dreams;

which is the very thing you are fighting to do. God will send you signs and markers that you are aligned with your purpose, in spite of contrary opinions; and that you are getting closer with every passing day to your breakthrough. The signs and markers are always present.

If you learn to see God, you will understand the blueprints to your destiny.

A Place of Arrival

I eventually finished writing my book; *The Universe Is Inviting You In*. Through another divine encounter, I was able to get Les Brown's testimonial on the front cover of my book. It reads, "*The Universe is Inviting You In,* is a great tool on the road to your destiny. Each of us must choose our path and utilize the knowledge and wisdom that is guiding our journey from within, giving us the power to live our dreams." –Les Brown (The Motivator)

Les Brown is the top African-American motivational speaker in the world. My purpose, as is yours, is greater than any opposition you will ever face en route to fulfilling your dreams. Days after my book was released, I ended up doing a book signing at a major networking event in Atlanta, GA. Les Brown was one of the speakers. I spent my twenty-fourth birthday taking a picture with Les Brown and giving him a printed copy of the book he was gracious enough to endorse for me.

Pay Attention

The universe will place images of who you are in front of you during your dream pursuit. You will encounter people who are doing what you aspire to do with your life. Do not take these moments lightly, and learn all you can in these instances through being humble enough to acknowledge the advantage of someone who is more seasoned and accomplished than you being in your presence. I found myself listening to Les Brown over the years and actually being in his presence on occasion. I was there to learn and be inspired when he spoke, but my greater purpose was to see how he did what he did to become a household staple in the self-development industry.

I would notice the subtle ways he sold his products during his speeches. I would notice how he offered multi layered programs to include everyone who wanted to go to the next level in their aspirations. I was noticing the unspoken conversation, which is the real conversation.

It's not about what people say; the truth of how people arrived at their various stations in life has everything to do with how they move and what they do.

Learn to notice the unspoken conversation when in the presence of greatness to bring clarity and focus to your own dream pursuit. Stay pliable and understand you'll never have it all figured out.

Your Instincts are Pivotal

During this season of separation, you want to understand how necessary it is for you to have great instincts, and how pivotal they are to your arrival at your promised land. I've seen many people have great work ethics and dedication thinking that was enough, only to take tremendous losses in business and in life. Work ethics and dedication are great, but your instincts are of greater importance. Dreams and purpose often turn into something that exists outside of the realm of a traditional nine to five job. It often becomes some sort of individual endeavor, where the safety net of human resources does not avail itself to you. Becoming independently successful places you in shark-infested waters, bringing about the need for superior instincts.

As you are in your season of separation and learning how your respective game is played, take the time to learn from your mistakes. You'll quickly learn that there aren't that many types of people. Take your findings and be selective about who can enter your space.

You are going to make many mistakes, but do your best to evolve from each misstep and allow that knowledge you gained to prevent you from making the same mistake again.

To be a successful dreamer, you have to get to the point that you know what people are going to do before they even know they're going to do it. You literally have to develop the ability to see around corners. When I mentor people, I often tell them that a large portion of my business is keeping things away from me that are not a match. My ability to stay in business is contingent upon my ability to assess people and situations very quickly. Human nature will reveal itself to you. Understand what type of people and situations bring you the outcomes and experiences you desire, and settle for nothing less than those experiences. If you do not develop your instincts, just as the aforementioned athletes mentioned earlier in the book, you could lose everything you worked for, in a matter of moments.

You have to feel your way through life as a successful dreamer. Trust the still small voice from within that speaks to you about people and situations. Your spirit is here to guide you. It will never lead you wrong. If something doesn't feel right, it usually is a detriment to you. You don't want to find yourself, after taking an unnecessarily tremendous loss, saying, "I knew something wasn't right." Too many of those moments and you'll be in difficult positions trying to recover from it all. Your instincts have to be your compass. Having been in a position where I've been living my dreams for many years, my gauge on a person's ability to succeed at certain endeavors is how intelligent they move and the strength of their instincts.

As you use this season of your dream pursuit to serve you and facilitate your season of uncommon success that is to follow. Towards the time when you are transitioning from the season of separation to accumulation, the severity of the resistance will heighten, and challenges will become more frequent and will arrive with increased fervor.

Breakthroughs

There are breakthroughs in life and life-altering breakthroughs in life. The trials I went through to get my book published culminated into a breakthrough. It was a blessing for my book to have as much backing and credibility as it did, but there was much more work that awaited me to facilitate a comfortable living solely living my dreams. The life-changing breakthroughs instantly change the complexion of your life. These breakthroughs elevate you to places you've imagined for yourself, but have yet to experience.

The opposition and challenges that precede this type of breakthrough are more intense than anything you've encountered. There are forces that do not want you to arrive at this place, and it will become very apparent in the abundance if illogical opposition you will face.

There was a year that changed the complexion of my life. Everything that I fought for happened. Everything that people told me, that they thought would never happen in my life, happened. Unfathomable blessings entered my space, and quickly. My life was progressively getting better, but one day I just went to a level that no other breakthroughs I'd experienced could rival.

This particular year there was a unified message that came to me from various people, some close and some not, "Matthew, you are less than. You aren't meeting your societal bench marks, and you will likely amount to nothing." This message came to me verbally as well as in the actions of people. It came in the form of family who had seen my steady and prolonged fight to live my dreams. It came in the form of a significant other who repeatedly told me I was not enough in various ways. Perfect strangers were greeting me with hostility at my public appearances. So much so, that I was forced to consult security firms for my own safety. This year was real.

This is a pivotal moment in your dream pursuit because opposition will come from places you never suspected it would. This is a blessing. This level of tribulation is evidence that you are close to your promised land. The life-altering breakthrough is eminent. The blessing resides in the reality that you have an opportunity to see people for who they are around you, and understand their true sentiment toward you. This occurs at this moment because God does not want you just to enter your Promised Land; He wants you to stay there without any detriments to your ability to reside there.

The best action you can undertake in this moment is to call black, black, and blue, blue. Do not rationalize anything that you see. Call it what it is and act accordingly. If you choose not to act, everything you fought for will be compromised.

There are people who know you deserve every blessing coming your way, but they'll do anything to sabotage your success and season of breakthrough because they told people you would never arrive there.

They would rather blatantly interfere with, and downplay your blessings, than to have to face the reality that they were wrong about you. This is deep.

You counter this by removing and restructuring relationships when you see this side of people. Their sentiments toward you are not going to change. They revealed their heart toward you. If you choose to keep them in your space, and consequently get burned down the line, take full responsibility for the repercussions. It was your fault.

Look at the timing of it all. Why so many people all of a sudden? It's because God is giving you a choice. When I eliminated everyone from my space that was against me, a strange thing happened, I was inundated with life-changing blessings that changed the complexion of my life. Change was instant, and since I have maintained the adjustments I had to make, I've resided on an elevated level of living. You will see things in people that you don't want to see, but becoming a successful dreamer is dependent upon you respecting what you see.

Accumulation

It's your "time" when an overwhelming amount of breakthroughs take place on your behalf, that logic cannot explain.

This is the moment when all of your efforts and God's favor converge and you are elevated to your next phase of blessing. In this stage of your dream pursuit, you are far from dreaming and living in the fullness of the reality of what was once a dream, and experiencing every blessing that defines this season. This is when the people who may have criticized your progression through life, look in awe of how you surpassed them. Your accumulations and possessions come effortlessly, as you are able to take full dominion over them. You are free to go about creating your day in whatever fashion you'd like to. There are countless avenues and opportunities for you to use your gifts to enhance the lives of others. You are in a flow of blessings. This is the place of accumulation.

Life is cyclical. Always remember that your Creator was always present and never forsook you, at any stage of life. Dream pursuits are encapsulated with highs and lows. Stay fixated in faith in every season, because ultimately, God's favor, which has been present in your life, will change any and every situation. Drown out the noises that don't align with your purpose and this singularity of vision will usher you to favorable places on the dance floor.

Notes and Insights

Notes and Insights

Chapter 8:

It Has Nothing to Do With You

*"Accept the perfection that is you,
in all of its totality and glory."*

-Matthew C. Horne

Years ago I went to see the James Brown biopic, "Get on Up." Aside from it being a masterful recount of the legendary entertainer James Brown's life, there was irrefutable revelation on life and its limitless nature that is available to us all, if we believe.

There was a scene in the movie where James was rehearsing a musical set his band had perfected exactly the way James wanted it. James then told his drummer to come into the set at a place in the song that wasn't musically correct. A band member challenged James on this and James told him,: "If it sounds good and it feels good, then it's musical." Leading up to this James said, "God made your ears! How are you going to argue with God's ears?"

Your Music Has an Audience

The next scene in the movie after the rehearsal scene was James Brown and his band playing the set the new way in front of a live audience. The audience was going crazy and was enamored with the new musical arrangement. The band member who challenged James on the sequence of the music and possible non-receptivity by listeners had nothing to do with what James knew regarding the way he heard the music internally. People will challenge the potential receptivity of your music if they think it's not musically inclined to the world's ear. Their concerns are mute.

> *When you continue to play your music exactly the way it is given to you, your encounter with your ordained audience is inevitable.*

It doesn't matter if people do not receive your music, because no one's music is universally accepted. Only be concerned with your match, the people who revere and celebrate your music. These people do exist and will show you the purpose of your music. If people don't receive your music, it's just not for them.

The most important factor in creating your music is being detached from how it will be received.

When you adopt the mindset that you will strictly create your music and stay detached from outcomes, you will master your music.

Only Consider Your Source

If you notice, James Brown never considered his audience; he only considered how he believed God was instructing him to play his music. The result was the audience receiving the best version of music that James could deliver to them. You water down your music when you consider your audience. The Creator of your music only instructs you to play it how it naturally comes to you; given that He has already, hand selected your audience members.

When you don't consider your audience when creating your music, you're serving them in the highest manner. You're giving them the best possible product, due to its' purity and divinity. You're giving them music from the Source of all sources, with no worldly interference. Play your music exactly as it is given to you, and consider nothing else.

Your Music Is Your Genius

This is one of the most powerful pieces of cinematography that I've ever seen. The essence of what James Brown said is that your music is greater than any natural laws that exist. It is given to you to play exactly the way it was given to you to play. James Brown was considered a musical genius because he had originality that captivated audiences for decades. He was himself. In being himself, he tapped into a genius, the genius that was he.

Many people never play their music because they have more faith in the world's rules, regulations, opinions, and statutes. Your music was given to you exclusively and never meant to be validated against anything other than the opinion of the Creator who gave you your music. He sees your music as pure perfection and genius because your music is a manifestation of Him.

No two people's music is exactly alike. No finite being created your music, so no finite being has the ability to quantify your notes as musically inclined or not.

When you have more faith in the opinions of others and self-doubt from within, you are choosing to argue with God.

God gave you one instruction with your music, to play it freely!

You can't validate a spiritual calling against rules and regulations rooted in this world.

This is attempting to serve two masters.

People miss their calling because they apply principles and precepts rooted in this world against the divine music that destiny is beckoning them to play.

As the bible speaks of, you cannot serve two masters. You will have to love one and despise the other. If you are going to experience the fullness of your gift, your eyes must stay fixated on the Creator and Conductor of your music, God.

I had a person ask me, "What validates you to be a motivational speaker?" This question lacked tact on many levels, given this person knew nothing about where I was in my career. I responded with, "God gave me a gift. People's lives have been changed by it. The end."

Meaningless Bells and Whistles

At the time of this person asking me this question, I'd written five books that sold globally, been publicly endorsed by the some of the top motivational speakers in the world, shared the stage with some of the top speakers in the world, written for the Washington Post Newspaper. I had my own television show that was featured in/on magazines, television, and radio. None of this crossed my mind when I was asked this question. My foremost thought was that my validation existed before I was ever manifested into this world, and that's the only validation I'll ever need in my lifetime.

> *When people ask you, "What makes you think you can do something?" You tell them, "Who makes you know you can do it?"*

You Don't Have To Ask

You don't have to ask for permission to live your dreams and purpose when you've been commissioned to live them before you ever arrived in this physical world. Seeking validation and permission is placing worldly parameters on your calling, stifling it. You were validated, qualified, and given permission to be your unique self by your Creator, who does not respect the laws of time and space because He is eternal. You are eternal.

> *If you maintain a God consciousness with your dream pursuit, then all your worldly roadblocks and challenges will have nothing to do with you.*

Your life has a great commission. This is your purpose. The purpose of this lifetime is to reconnect to whatever you were purposed to do and be, before you ever showed up here. This is mission you were given which facilitated your arrival in this realm. The success of your mission depends on whether you will agree to it. That is why you've been commissioned, because the effectiveness of your mission requires you to actively participate in creating it. There are two parties: you and God. Other voices are going to speak to you, but only one must call your name.

Claim Your Life

About a year ago, I had a conversation with a young woman about the state of her life. It was in chaos. She was unhappy in virtually every facet of her life. She was stressed on a job that was more like a battleground. Her stress was leading to depression and unwanted weight gain. Her life imbalance could be traced directly to her job and mounting debts that required her to work at this job, along with other responsibilities.

She had things she wanted to do with her life, but the opinions of others lauded about what a great job she had, and not to forfeit such an opportunity even if it was dismantling her from the inside out. She stayed in an unhappy position due to the opinions of other people until she nearly broke down to the point of needing professional help.

She had aspirations that would completely remove her from her job and afford her the opportunity to make a living on her terms, with a life of balance and peace. My advice was to stop living for other people and to acknowledge what this way of living has gotten her. It dawned on me that this young woman needed to reclaim her life. I advised her to identify every facet of her life that was imbalanced and lacked fulfillment, and to identify what would bring her fulfillment in those areas of her life. Furthermore, I admonished her to devise actions that would facilitate her having success in the areas of life that she was lacking in, and to not stop moving towards this reframed life until she had the fulfillment she desired. If she accepted the reality of what must be done to reclaim her life, then her life would fashion itself into the beauty she desired.

The best way to construct your life is to claim it. If you claim your life, you will never have to reclaim it.

As it relates to what brings you fulfillment in life, focus on those things and nothing else. Embrace the blank canvas that your life truly is. Paint your vision on life's canvas. Paint your vision and no one else's. I am living life freely now because I chose to claim my life, and do away with opinions and tactics that were designed to dissuade me from fulfilling my purpose. My music spoke louder that contrary voices, and I was able to claim my life with no interruption, and frame my world how I envisioned it being.

Reclaim Your Life

Many people wake up discontent, realizing that they've been living for other people, creating an imbalanced life. Reclaiming your life is more difficult than claiming your life, but the difficulty must not be the focus, only the reality that you must reframe the important areas of your life if you are ever to experience fulfillment and balance. If this is your life situation, I implore you to reclaim your existence. It is possible because you are breathing. There is contentment with reclaiming your life, even as you take the steps to do so, knowing you are giving yourself a fighting chance to frame your world the way you envisioned for yourself.

If you surrender your life to anything other than your purpose, you will feel the void of not being what you were designed to be.

Even with missteps being taken in life, it's never over if you are breathing.

Your Creator is more concerned with you doing what He purposed you to do in the earth, than with punishing you. God is constantly posturing you to align with your life's design, with the hope that you will agree to your mission.

Whatever direction you are being nudged to go in, just say, "Yes." All you have to do is say, "Yes."

Notes and Insights

Notes and Insights

CHAPTER 9:

IT'S BIGGER THAN YOU

"You are a gift to be given in any time, situation, or circumstance."

-MATTHEW C. HORNE

Years ago, I was out of the country celebrating my birthday. It was a great time, and on the second day, my brother's friend arrived. This man and I sat down for lunch and began to converse. He was having some relationship issues with his then girlfriend who is now his wife. I listened intently as the man told me how things were transpiring in his relationship. I was able to make some deductions and conclusions about the circumstances based on my understanding of male and female interaction, as well as my understanding of human nature.

I said to the man, "When she did this, you did this. When you did this, she did this." He responded with, "How in the world did you know that?" I told him that I had just written and released my latest book, *How To Get Beautiful Women ....and Everything Else You Want From Life*, and that I had observed male-female interaction for years and had a very firm grasp on the underlying motives and behaviors that transpire in these situations. I gave him advice on what he should do, and he ceaselessly expressed his gratitude. I could tell in his reaction that he had been intently searching for the answers he received in our conversation. He then asked me, "How much is your book? Do you have any copies here?"

I didn't have any copies because I left the country to have fun and get away from everything. Essentially, I was, "Off." I went back to my room and meditated on this encounter. I came to three life-changing conclusions:

1. Your Gifts Are the Solutions You Were Sent Here To Deliver To Your Fellow Man
2. Your Prosperity Is In Your Gifts
3. You Should Never Shelve Your Gifts

Deliver Your Solutions

The man in the above example received a solution that he had been longing for based on me operating in my gift.

There are many people who you will be a savior to their situation, and solution to their problems, if you choose to operate in your gifts.

You are a literal solution personified. We're all here for each other. Please do not minimize your gifts and their potential to change the complexion of someone's life. There is unlimited power in what you have to deliver to this world. Actively participate in being the breakthrough your fellow man needs to experience.

The beauty in your gifts is that there are people who are designed to encounter your gift because you are their solutions. I've ran into people who I haven't seen in years and was able to share wisdom with them that was pivotal to their season in life, while giving them peace about how their life events were transpiring. Even if fear surrounds operating in your gifts and the corresponding outcomes, please find peace knowing that the universe has people hand-selected to receive what you offer.

You owe it to God to deliver your gifts, given that He freely gave them to you with the intention that you would freely operate in them to enhance the lives of your fellow man.

Prosperity

In the above example, it is very evident that your prosperity is in your gifts, given that after he received the solution he was searching for he asked how much my book cost. He would have paid anything for my book in that moment given the gravity of the solution he received from me. Notice, after the solution was delivered, the opportunity for financial exchange immediately presented itself. People spend money daily for solutions. The more valuable of a solution it is, the more monetary exchange is involved. Your prosperity is in your gifts, because your gifts are the greatest and purest solutions you have to offer to the world. This, in turn, will provide you with the greatest returns in life. Your prosperity is no further than you freely operating in your gifts.

Change Your Financial Situation

You may be in a financially destitute situation or heading towards one; there is an escape. I've experienced and witnessed it repeatedly throughout the years. During the last government shutdown, two women who personified the ability to change your situation, instantly, through imposing their will on life, and not accepting what was in front of them in the way of dire and widespread financial crisis. They took action in what would turn out to be the longest government shutdown in history.

These sisters were from my hometown of Fort Washington, Maryland. They were both government workers with no paycheck and bills that didn't respect a government shutdown. The sisters began baking and selling cheesecakes to make financial ends meet. Their cheesecake business gained immediate momentum when superstar comedian and television show host, Ellen DeGeneres, publicly endorsed their cheesecake business by infusing twenty thousand dollars into it, and tasting a piece of their cheesecake on live television. When this happened, the sisters were inundated and overwhelmed with orders on a national and international scale. The sisters both quit their full time government jobs to run their bourgeoning business. This all culminated into their cheesecakes being sold in select Walmart stores.

You are never without the tools to create your way out of any situation if you choose to take inventory of your gifts. Accept the reality of what must be done to make your gifts of monetary value and you will posture yourself to receive prosperity.

Never Shelve Your Gifts

You should never shelve any gift because of the potential of it, and the design behind it.

This brings my three realizations from the beginning of the chapter full circle. You should never shelve your gifts because they are the solutions you were sent here to deliver to your fellow man.

The Power in Wisdom

Gifts are not just the innate things that we do effortlessly. Gifts also manifest themselves in the form of transferrable wisdom from our experiences. This is meant to be shared as well. Share all forms of your gifts, freely.

I'm addressing this in my next book, that I am writing to young black women on how to posture themselves to be prepared for the good black men they encounter. There is an epidemic of non-black marriage amongst women taking place, of the latest statistic being that only twenty-eight percent of black women are being projected to ever be married. I became aware of this statistic when watching ESPN's Chris Broussard speak on the subject matter. I trust this statistic because his career is based on statistical analysis, as well as journalistic integrity and prowess. I'm a proponent of black love and black marriage, and want to do my part to bridge the marriage gap that exists in the black race.

One thing I mention in the book is how the elder black women could use their experiences with men, even if they ultimately were eluded by the outcomes they wanted from these interactions in their lifetime, to share with the younger black women to increase their chances of creating favorable outcomes with the good men they encounter. I've witnessed mothers intentionally enacting sabotage attempts to get their daughters away from good men so they won't be overshadowed by the daughters success. The need for the gift of wisdom from the elder women in the black community to end the cycle of non-marriage is eminent. There's a gift in the wisdom of experience from the things we've even gotten wrong in life.

    The gift of the wisdom of experience is not to be taken lightly. You could be a seasoned athlete who sees some young athletes in your sport of expertise and choose to give them tips. You could have ties to a prestigious university and help a young, hardworking, kid gain admittance to the institution through your connections. You can be a seasoned nurse and propel the next generation of nurses in their careers through your wisdom. Respect all forms of the gifts you were given, and honor the intent behind them, which is to leave your fellow man better than how you encountered them.

Notes and Insights

Notes and Insights

Chapter 10:

A Woman Named Susan

"Life-altering breakthroughs manifest themselves through encounters, people, and moments."

Years ago, I was working a non-committal full time type of job. I had authored three books and was taking motivational speaking gigs as they came. I did book signings every weekend I could, often finding myself working seven days a week to pay my bills, as well as to fulfill my dreams.

There came a day at the job I was working where I knew my time was up. The realization came in an instant, as I knew I'd experienced my last day at this place. I said, "I'm never doing this again." This is the last day I ever worked a job. I didn't have a sizable amount of money saved. I just knew it was my time to go all in with my purpose and dreams.

Right on cue, I did two books signings that weekend. Products that didn't normally sell did and I experienced a prosperous weekend. One woman purchased a sizeable amount of books for herself and others she had in mind. This woman's name was Susan. Susan and I talked and she was totally behind a young man doing what I was doing, and said she would continue to support my work. Susan contacted me soon after my book signing that weekend and said she had been telling people about me. Susan went all over DC to people she knew, in addition to total strangers, telling them about the young motivational speaker she met, in addition to the nature of his books. She literally started taking book orders on the spot from people she was encountering daily.

Susan would call me every week and have me deliver the books to her that people had purchased, and I would sign each copy to whoever made the purchase. Susan would just give me the money. This went on for weeks, and I was beyond thankful to her for doing this. Susan was an angel. She had no idea how timely she was in my life. Susan was a major factor in my ability to hold on financially as I figured things out after leaving the job I was working.

Susan and I would talk regularly. In doing so, she let me know that she was putting together a conference in Washington, D.C. and inviting some retired NBA and NFL stars who both became pastors to speak at her event. This was exciting, and my only planned involvement was to attend the event. One day Susan asked me if I would like to speak at this event. She was intent on highlighting talent from all over, both known and unknown. I responded with, "Yes." Susan made a substantial investment in me for this event and I was able to share the stage with a lineup of powerful speakers.

This was the beginning of me entering into my season of accumulation and prosperity. I was obedient to what I instinctively knew to do, even when all of the natural indicators showed it wouldn't be the best move to stop working with no money saved. My waters were ruffling and I trusted the Source of All Creation over every reality that was in front of me. My life has never been the same since I walked away from that job. I have no negative feelings toward the employment I once held. I am thankful for the experiences I had, and the people I was able to meet. Life has been full of freedom and prosperity ever since I made that decision to trust God, when the timing made no natural sense in accordance with what I was being compelled to do.

Bells and Whistles or Signs and Markers

We have the choice to align our lives and make sure every bell and whistle is in place, before we follow our instincts, or we can go with the signs and markers, which indicate something is formulating spiritually on our behalf. Upon arrival at your finished line, you will see what was brewing all along.

I didn't just come up with the material for this book from nowhere. I went through all of the stages of the dream pursuit, and these are my findings.

Your Source has it all figured out and needs you to align with the destiny that was prepared for you.

There are many "Susan's" in place to assist you when you make the decision to move in the direction you feel compelled to move. I was just watching an interview with Byron Allen, the black entertainment billionaire mogul. This interview took place on the Breakfast Club Radio Show. Byron Allen talked about how he called every major television network and attempted to sell his comedic interview style television show to them. Every door repeatedly shut in his face, as network owner after network owner refused to entertain the idea of his show, and give him the opportunity to be a part of their network. Byron was selling his television show to the networks for free, which is unheard of given that television networks pay for television shows to be on their network. His idea was to sell advertisement spots during the commercials on his show and actually allow the networks to take half of the advertisement time and sell it themselves to make a profit from his show.

Byron Allen essentially said I'll pay you to be on your network, and the doors continually slammed in his face, due to his race. His idea was brilliant. Byron Allen, being well connected with famous comedians, had the household names to command viewership of his shows. Certain people in power didn't want to see him succeed.

One day Byron Allen received a call from a media mogul by the name of Roger King. This man distributed television shows, just as Byron Allen did. Roger King was a mega wealthy television industry mogul, while Bryon was attempting to establish his footing in the television industry. Roger King told Byron Allen to fly out to Los Angeles and pitch him on the show he was selling. Roger was very impressed with Byron and his ability to sell. He told Byron Allen that the television network executives that he regularly interacted with were intentionally not returning his calls because of his race.

Roger had leverage on all of these executives with Roger owning television shows such as "The Price is Right."

and "The Oprah Winfrey Show." The television stations needed Roger much more than he needed them. Roger King detested the racial discrimination of a man who called these executives from sun up to sun down, only to be ignored. Roger King was having an event at his house and all of the television executives who ignored Byron Allen would be in attendance. Roger King instructed Byron Allen to show up at this event. When Byron Allen showed up the day of the event, Roger King began to pull all of the television executives who ignored Byron Allen to the side and said, "If you want my shows on your network for renewal, you have to do business with Byron Allen."

Byron Allen said the complexion of his life changed after that day. He never had a problem getting his shows on any of the major television networks and ultimately became a billionaire player in the entertainment game.

Fully Engaged

One of the most memorable parts of the interview is that Byron Allen financed the production of his show with his own money. He said he was repeatedly late on his mortgage and did not eat some days because all of his resources were allocated to fulfilling his dream. Not every dream pursuit will require this exact level of sacrifice, but every dream pursuit has a level of sacrifice built into it.

Your success is in observing the reality of what it takes to fulfill your dreams, and not relenting until you arrive at your destination.

This is what dreams are made of.

You have to ask yourself if you are willing to go to the necessary lengths required to fulfill your dreams. This is what I mean by accepting every reality that comes along with fulfilling your dreams, for better and for worse.

"Susan" Will Appear

"Susan," and whether she will appear, is the main contributing factor to people not pursuing their dreams. People want so much control over their future and the ability to dictate outcomes, that they never even engage the idea of pursuing their dreams, because of the overabundance of unknown variables involved.

You have to surrender to meet "Susan." The encounters that will tie every loose end and catapult you to unthinkable realms of success are on your path if you choose to undertake your dream pursuit. Surrendering your dream to the Source of All Creation is your greatest asset as you pursue your dreams and create the life you envision for yourself.

The Highest Floor in the Building

I can equate life to a building. There's a floor with fear. There's a floor with doubt. There's a floor with opposition. There's a floor with possibility. The floor with possibility exists because you have a God consciousness and understand that nothing life throws your way is beyond resolution from your Creator.

You're going to face unexpected and unfavorable circumstances in life. You will have aspirations that will require you to surrender control of the outcomes of your life, given the many unknowns that contribute to the arrival at the place you see vividly from within. Your quality of life is dependent on which floor you choose to reside on in this building of life.

It's natural to make a stop on one of the lesser floors because we are human beings with human nature. We all experience fear and doubt, in addition to finding ourselves staggered by opposition. When you master your life and consistently get the outcomes that you desire from life, you only make temporary stops on these floors when it comes to the many facets of life and aspirations, while opting to continue to venture to the top floor and reside there.

God consciousness is essentially life-mastery. I say this because when you move through life with a God consciousness you won't feel the full gravity of whatever life throws your way, because you know there is always an avenue of escape. You immediately consider what the Source has to say about any life circumstance, as opposed to wallowing in the fear of seemingly insurmountable obstacles. This creates perspective in any circumstance. This perspective leads you to the Source who has any and all resolutions for you because He created you. God has the ultimate final say regarding anything any of His creations will ever encounter.

Choose to occupy the highest floor in the building and times of tumult will be accompanied by unwavering peace.

Notes and Insights

Notes and Insights

About The Author

Matthew C. Horne, motivational speaker and author, is the president of Optimum Success International, a speaking and publishing company located in the metropolitan Washington, DC area. He is an international authority on Maximizing Human Potential. Matthew is the author of *The Universe Is Inviting You In*, and *All We Have Is NOW*, which are both publicly endorsed by legendary motivational speaker Les Brown. He is also the author of *Choices: The Young Black Man's Guide to Successful Living*, *How to Get Beautiful Women …and Everything Else You Want From Life*, and *The Successful Dreamer*. Growing up, Matthew's ultimate vision for his life was to play basketball in the NBA. He positioned himself to live this reality through obtaining a full-athletic scholarship to play Division I basketball in college. Much to his surprise destiny revealed his true calling during his collegiate years, as he discovered a passion for motivational speaking.

About the Author

Matthew was told by his professors he would never make it as an English major, and to the astonishment of everyone, he not only obtained a Bachelor of Arts Degree in English, but also was offered his first book contract before he graduated in his last semester of college. Matthew's message is one of creating your own reality according to your vivid destiny pictures. Matthew empowers audiences to live their unique truth, independent of the opinions of others. Matthew's message is quickly spanning the globe through his books, audios, and motivational speeches. He has served as a guest-columnist for the *Washington Post's* "The Root DC" section. He is the creator of the television show "Matthew C. Horne Live!" He has also been featured on the legendary radio station WOL with his weekly minute motivational segments. Matthew also owns Lightning Fast Book Publishing, a company that publishes author's books in three weeks. Matthew C. Horne also owns *Matthew C. Horne Author PR, Marketing, and Management*, a company that provides a full range of public relations services for authors of any genre. Matthew is available for speeches, radio and television interviews, and book signings. All who encounter Matthew C. Horne, will leave with a heightened awareness of their limitless possibilities, and be positioned to live their Best Life Possible. To learn more about Matthew C. Horne, please visit www.matthewchorne.com.

Matthew C. Horne's Additional Titles

Available at www.matthewchorne.com

SERVICES

Motivational Speaking/Book Publishing/ Public Relations for Authors

Motivational Speaking: Matthew C. Horne is the world's premier motivational speaker and leading authority in Maximizing Human Potential. His message has spanned the globe and will bring any audience to life through an awareness of their limitless possibilities and creative potential. Matthew is available for speeches, lectures, seminars, radio, and television interviews.

Testimonial: Thank you very much for your recent motivational speech on "Peak Performance in the Workplace." I am very appreciative of what you delivered to our employees here at NASA Goddard Space Flight Center.

You brought your experience to the table and stressed teamwork. Your entire presentation was value-added. In a brief period of time, you stressed how employees can achieve peak performance by valuing their work and bringing their best work and attitude to everything they attempt.

—Michael P. Kelly
Chief, Institutional Support Office,
NASA Goddard Space Flight Center

Book Publishing

Matthew C. Horne's book publishing company, *Lightning Fast Book Publishing* is a full service book publishing company, which produces books, and builds the author's overall platform to become a reputable public figure. Matthew's company has a personal touch, as he is heavily involved in the production of every author's book, and implements the same strategies for book production and distribution that are responsible for Matthew's decade plus long career as a successful globally selling author. Services range from book editing, cover design to website design and global sales and distribution for author's books. To learn more about *Lightning Fast Book Publishing* please visit www.lfbookpublishing.com.

Testimonial: The Lightning Fast Book Publishing Team over delivered in their publishing of my book, "G.R.A.C.E: God's Reconstruction After Cancer Exits." My fully designed, edited, and printed book was finished in two-and a-half weeks. The symbolism on the book cover captured my books' content in totality. Lightning Fast Book Publishing is the premier company for all of your book publishing needs!

Bonnie Crittendon-Powell, Author of "Grace: God's Reconstruction After Cancer Exits"

Public Relations for Authors

Matthew C. Horne Author PR, Marketing and Management is a Public Relations company that specializes exclusively in promoting authors. Every author receives a tailored Public Relations strategy to get each author to his or her desired outcome as an author. Matthew's experience with having publicists in the past has been all excuses and no results. Matthew C. Horne served as his own PR, Marketing, and Management team throughout the years, culminating into a very successful career entrenched in longevity. Matthew C. Horne recreates this experience for every author he represents. For more information, please visit www.matthewchorneauthorpr.com.

Testimonial: When it came to marketing my novels, there were those who promised me the world, but it was Matthew C. Horne Author PR, Marketing and Management that actually brought the dream to reality. This company coached me with excellent strategies for selling, put me in touch with outstanding entrepreneurs, increased my book signing events tremendously, and supplied engagements on both radio and internet shows where I gained world-wide exposure. Today, I can honestly say that I am selling far more books than ever before, and, with the help of this company, I am in touch with a community of business people who continue to connect with me in a multiplicity of ways. Matthew C. Horne commandeers a superb company that guarantees excellence and makes no excuse for anything less.

Doris H. Dancy, Author
The Redemptive Love Series:
Jagged Edges
Shattered Pieces
All Other Ground

CPSIA information can be obtained
at www.ICGtesting.com
Printed in the USA
JSHW020026150422
24841JS00004B/52